MORNINGS WITH THE HOLY SPIRIT

A 42-Day Journey of Prayer, Fasting, and Consecration with the Holy Spirit for Accelerating Your Life and Fulfilling Your Destiny

Charlene Vassell-Wright

Mornings with the Holy Spirit: *A 42-Day Journey of Prayer, Fasting, and Consecration with the Holy Spirit for Accelerating Your Life and Fulfilling Your Destiny*

Copyright @ 2024 Charlene Vassell-Wright

Published 2024.

All rights reserved.

ISBN: 979-8-218-35979-9

Library of Congress Control Number: 2024900967

The contents of this devotional may not be replicated or reproduced in any form without the publisher's written consent.

Scripture quotations taken from The Holy Bible, New International Version® NIV®. Copyright © 1973, 1978, 1984, 2011 by Biblica, Inc. Used with permission. All rights reserved worldwide.

"Many are the plans in a person's heart, but it is the Lord's purpose that prevails."

(Proverbs 19:21)

Dedication

I humbly dedicate this devotional to the Almighty God, who deserves all honor and glory. With deep gratitude and reverence, I offer this work back to Him, knowing that He will get the credit for the many lives this devotional will touch, heal, bless, and transform.

To my loving husband Congdon, daughter Liana, and mother Kareen, your unwavering patience, love, understanding, and support throughout my time of consecration have been invaluable.

To the incredible members of the 'Too Much to Gain to Lose' prayer group, I extend my heartfelt gratitude. Your unwavering faith, encouragement, and prayers have been instrumental in helping me birth this long-awaited publication.

May this devotional be a testament to the power of the Holy Spirit, guiding readers toward a deeper connection with God and a transformative spiritual journey. May it bring healing, blessings, and transformation to the lives of those who read its pages, and may God's love and grace shine through every word.

Acknowledgment

To Trish Chin, my prayer partner, destiny helper, friend, and editor. Our mornings in prayer and conversations with the Holy Spirit have served as a foundation for this book.

I appreciate your meticulous attention to detail and how you've pushed me to enhance this manuscript to its fullest potential. Your essence truly reflects the spirit of a supportive sister who looks out for the best interests of others.

Praise for the Work

In witnessing the remarkable journey of a person achieving a milestone, it's easy to revel in the celebratory moments. However, what often remains unseen is the profound backstory that only a privileged few are fortunate enough to witness. I count myself among those with the distinct privilege of having a front-row seat to the transformative power unleashed when one seeks God's will for their life and embraces the abundant fruits born out of sacrificial dedication.

In a society defined by instant gratification and the pursuit of personal desires, we find ourselves ensconced in a microcosm where things swiftly align with our wishes. However, Charlene's story stands out as an inspiring testament to the potency of obedience to the divine call, even amidst the tumultuous storms of life. I observed her navigate the unpredictable ebbs and flows of her journey, a journey marked by a profound transformation process.

Emerging from the crucible of a 42-day consecration, Charlene emerged not just changed but utterly transformed—a woman wholly surrendered to the intricate plans divinely laid out for her life. Though a mere scratch on the surface, this devotional offers a glimpse into the depth of Charlene's spiritual journey. With a discerning ear attuned to the whispers of the Holy Spirit, Charlene unfolds the mysteries and intricacies of divine guidance with a rare clarity that resonates profoundly.

Trish Chin, writer and editor of *Unabridged! Magazine*

Welcome to this Devotional Journey

Here is your invitation to a sacred communion with the Holy Spirit. Here, you are offered an exclusive pass to witness some of my most enlightening and transformative conversations with God. In 2023– from August to October, I had some extraordinary conversations with God. **Yes! God still speaks.** I did not want to keep to myself the profound insights that changed so much of my perspective, so I have decided to share them with you.

But back to this devotional and why it might be beneficial to you. By the time this devotional is launched, the new year, 2024, will already be in swing. The time is ripe for aligning your goals and dreams with the plans of God for your life. This devotional might just be the start to aligning your plans with God's plan for your life.

This devotional was created for committing time to consecration and communion with the Holy Spirit, who sustains every aspect of your life—your destiny, purpose, mind, spirit, body, wealth, health, future, plans, goals, family, ministry, and business. This commitment is the bedrock upon which you build a foundation of courage, resilience, and structure.

You might ask, 'What is consecration, and how does it integrate into my life?' Let me explain. Consecration is the deliberate allocation of time for a higher purpose. In this context, it is about devoting time to listening to God. It is carving out moments from the hustle of life for prayer, fasting, worship, or distancing oneself from social engagements.

Consecration creates the atmosphere for clarity (clear instructions and directions of your visions); it allows time for self-reflection, which prompts you to do a root cause analysis of the recurrent problems you are facing or issues hindering you from progressing. It empowers self-confidence and belief once you become aware of your existing potential and purpose.

The genesis of this devotional traces back to August 2023, when I joined like-minded believers in forming a prayer circle called 'Too Much to Gain to Lose.' Our purpose was to respond to a call for help, reigniting the divine calling of a spiritual brother. Before the fasting and prayer ended, this brother experienced some of the greatest blessings he had ever experienced.

For 42 days, we fervently sought the Lord's will through prayer and fasting. We witnessed miracles and answered prayers, a testament to the profound power of prayer. I am eager to share this, so I invite you on a journey of prayer, fasting, and consecration with the Holy Spirit to accelerate your life and fulfill your destiny.

Let us make this devotional the start to nurturing and enriching you—attending to your emotional, spiritual, financial, and relational growth. I witnessed a radical transformation in 2023 and am excited about God's plans and purposes for me this season. My prayer is that you will, too.

This devotional is not a catch-all to the many challenges you will face but a particularly useful tool in keeping God at the center of your life, and it culminates with a closer walk with God. Prosperity is destined for everyone but guaranteed to those who intentionally work toward it.

This devotional was designed to be an interactive guide steering you toward success. **I hope you are ready!**

Before you begin, there are instructions. Yes, action items for you.
Ready? **Let's go!**

Instructions

1. Plan your consecration time deliberately—avoid distractions!

2. Aim for 42 days of fasting, if possible, respecting your health conditions. Fasting isn't obligatory but enriches your experience.

3. Consider a water-only or strict fast (no food or drink) daily from 6 am to 6 pm—**prioritize health; seek medical advice before you attempt any fast.**

4. Allocate 30 minutes to an hour each morning, ideally at 5 am or 6 am, providing this fits your life situation.

5. Look for a quiet, distraction-free environment for undisturbed worship and focus.

6. Have a Bible (The New International Version was used in this devotional, but any accessible version works) to reference during this journey.

7. You can use a journal to document experiences and insights—you'll encounter divine revelations. Alternatively, there is space provided in this devotional to document your thoughts.

8. You can undertake this journey solo or invite a prayer partner or group to harness the power of meaningful connections.

9. Keep inspirational worship music within reach.

10. Approach this journey with an open heart, the right mindset, and an expectation to be transformed and guided by the Holy Spirit.

About Mornings with the Holy Spirit: Your 42-Day Journey

This devotional is a pathway to a deeper connection with the Holy Spirit, a closer walk with God, and practical strategies for navigating life's twists, achieving meaningful success, and living an inspired and purpose-driven life.

Have you ever felt that inner tug urging you to deepen your relationship with God and uncover His purpose for your life? Perhaps you have yearned for a closer bond with the Holy Spirit, craving God's wisdom, guidance, and power in your daily walk. If so, this devotional was crafted just for you.

Discover tools and strategies for a 42-day journey of consecration, prayer, and fasting alongside the Holy Spirit. This intentional period of surrender and seeking God's presence promises to transform your spiritual walk and how you navigate your life.

Rooted in the author's personal surrender to the Holy Spirit, this devotional emerges from her journey—transitioning from a successful nursing career to becoming an entrepreneur and certified Christian life coach. She intimately understands the challenges and uncertainties entwined with answering God's call.

This devotional contains carefully chosen Bible verses from the author's studies, accompanied by her insights, wisdom, and strategies. These will shepherd you through a faith-infused journey marked by discipline and consistency.

Expect newfound clarity and direction through daily readings, prayers, and journal prompts. The Holy Spirit will unveil divine strategies, enabling you to conquer hurdles, embrace your identity in Christ, and fulfill your God-given purpose.

Whether you are seeking financial breakthroughs, liberation from self-defeating behaviors, or a deeper spiritual journey, 'Mornings with the Holy Spirit' offers practical counsel and spiritual sustenance. It is a wellspring to draw from while navigating life's ebbs and flows, assured that the Holy Spirit walks alongside you.

Are you ready to embark on this transformative journey? Open your heart, carve out dedicated time each morning, and allow the Holy Spirit to lead you toward heightened consecration, prayer, and fasting. Brace yourself to soar in life and destiny, aligning with God's purpose.

May this devotional ignite your spiritual growth, serve as an inspiration, and guide you toward experiencing the bountiful blessings of God. Let us take this step together, knowing that the Holy Spirit awaits, ready to transform us from within.

THE JOURNEY BEGINS...

Day One: Overcoming Negative Thoughts

"We demolish arguments and every pretension that sets itself up against the knowledge of God, and we take captive every thought to make it obedient to Christ." (2 Corinthians 10:5, NIV)

Further Reading: 2 Corinthians 10

Good morning! Have you ever had a weird thought that came out of nowhere? Believe me, that thought did not come out of midair. You see, our minds hold the key to our success or failure. How we perceive life impacts its quality. Our thoughts, beliefs, and attitudes shape the boundaries of what we perceive as possible and what we perceive as true. Not every thought is true. **Ouch!**

Aligning our thoughts with God's Word is a potent method to nurture a positive and empowering mindset. The Bible offers wisdom, guidance, and promises capable of transforming and aligning our thinking with God's truth. By immersing ourselves in the Word, we gain deeper insights into our identity, purpose, and the boundless potential within us through Christ.

For genuine transformation, it is crucial to identify and dismantle strongholds that hinder our progress. Procrastination, imposter syndrome, fear of failure, limited thinking, and a fixed mindset are common strongholds that restrain us from realizing our full potential. By acknowledging these negative patterns and actively striving to overcome them, we liberate ourselves from their grasp and embrace a mindset of growth, resilience, and faith.

Renewing our mindset is an ongoing process that demands intentional effort. It entails replacing negative thoughts and beliefs with positive and empowering ones. Practices like affirmations, visualization, gratitude, prayer, and immersing ourselves in positive influences aid this transformation.

By consistently aligning our thoughts with God's truth and dismissing limiting beliefs, we create fertile ground for personal growth and success. Our thoughts shape our actions, and our actions dictate our outcomes. Cultivating a mindset rooted in faith, possibility, and God's promises unlocks a realm of opportunities and breakthroughs. We begin to see ourselves as God sees us—owning our unlimited potential and ability to achieve extraordinary things.

Steps to Overcoming Challenges and Negative Thoughts through God's Power:

1. **Identify the Strongholds:** Begin your journaling journey by identifying the strongholds hindering your spiritual growth or relationship with God. Reflect on thoughts or beliefs limiting you from living a fulfilling life.

2. **Seek Divine Help:** Acknowledge your limited strength and seek God's guidance, wisdom, and strength to overcome these challenges.

3. **Challenge Negative Thoughts:** Write down negative thoughts conflicting with God's truth. Counter these thoughts with relevant scriptures and meditate upon them.

4. **Take Every Thought Captive:** Become aware of your thoughts. Write down negative ones and replace them with positive, God-centered thoughts.

5. **Align with Christ:** Reflect on aligning thoughts, actions, and obedience with Christ. Envision practical steps to honor Him daily.

6. **Understand Disobedience:** Ponder the repercussions of disobedience and align your actions with God's will.

Prayer: Dear God, help me to take stock of my thoughts. I surrender all negative thoughts to obeying who you are and the truth of your Word.

Insight: Incorporate these strategies into your journaling practice to deepen your understanding of 2 Corinthians 10. Seek God's guidance, rely on His power, and align your thoughts and actions with His truth.

Date: _____

Reflection or Thoughts:

(Start writing your reflections, thoughts, prayers, or anything you wish to journal about in the space below.)

Day Two: Embracing Challenges

"After this, the Moabites and Ammonites with some of the Meunites came to wage war against Jehoshaphat."
(2 Chronicles 20:1, NIV)

Further Reading: 2 Chronicles 20:1-25

Good morning! At some point in our lives, we will face adversity or challenges, but even those challenges come to teach us something. The verses in 2 Chronicles 20:1-25 chronicle a pivotal moment in ancient Judah's history when King Jehoshaphat confronted a daunting alliance of enemies. What adversaries are you currently facing in your life? Who or what stands in the way of your progress or success? Before blaming others, let us look at the man in the mirror.

Let's uncover the crucial elements and strategies to conquer your adversaries. Let's dive into this narrative:

1. **Context:** King Jehoshaphat, known for his unwavering faithfulness to God, was at the helm of Judah's rule. During this period, the Moabites, Ammonites, and Meunites formed a strong coalition that severely threatened Judah.

2. **Jehoshaphat's Reaction:** Confronted with this impending danger, King Jehoshaphat was alarmed and sought divine guidance. He proclaimed a fast throughout the land, rallying the people in Jerusalem to seek God's intervention.

3. **Jehoshaphat's Prayer:** In a heartfelt prayer, Jehoshaphat acknowledged God's supreme authority and recalled His historical aid to his ancestors. He expressed their reliance on God and their unwavering trust in His promises.

4. **God's Response:** Through the prophet Jahaziel, God assured Jehoshaphat and his people that the battle was not theirs but the Lord's. They were urged not to fear or despair, as God Himself would fight on their behalf.

5. **Worship and Adoration:** The next day, Jehoshaphat encouraged the people to have faith in God's promise. He appointed singers to lead the army, exalting God's holiness and unfailing love.

6. **Divine Intervention:** God set an ambush against the enemy alliance as the people sang and praised. Miraculously, the Moabites and Ammonites turned on each other, leading to their mutual destruction.

7. **Spoils of Triumph:** Jehoshaphat and his forces reached the vantage point to witness a scene of utter devastation. The adversaries lay defeated, and the spoils of war, including valuable possessions and livestock, lay in abundance.

8. **Gratitude and Festivity:** The people of Judah rejoiced, offering gratitude to God for His faithfulness and deliverance. They returned to Jerusalem with jubilation, celebrating their victory for three days.

Here's what I hope you takeaway from this story: running to God should be your first response. This story further elucidates the potency of prayer, faith, and praise when confronted with overwhelming challenges. King Jehoshaphat's humble reliance on God and the unity of the people in worship led to a miraculous triumph. It is a reminder that when we turn to God, acknowledging His sovereignty and trusting in His promises, He intervenes in extraordinary ways to overcome our adversaries. This narrative encourages us to confront our challenges with faith, prayer, and praise, understanding that God can bring deliverance and victory into our lives. **God got you!**

Prayer: Dear God, help me to remember that the challenges I face are yours– apart of your plans to perfect my life. May your Holy Spirit restrain me from fighting a battle you have already won.

Insight: On day two of the consecration, I sensed the Lord saying, "An abundance of blessings awaits you—more than you can carry." I profoundly felt this sense of not only provision but abundance from God, my provider on this day, but I had to get to the place of believing. I pray you will come into the fullness of God's provisions.

Date: _____

Reflection or Thoughts:

(Start writing your reflections, thoughts, prayers, or anything you wish to journal about in the space below.)

_____
_____
_____
_____
_____
_____
_____
_____
_____
_____
_____
_____
_____
_____
_____
_____
_____
_____
_____
_____
_____
_____
_____
_____
_____

Day Three: Embracing Unfinished Endeavors

"Being confident of this, that he who began a good work in you will carry it on to completion until the day of Christ Jesus."
(Philippians 1:6, NIV)

Further Reading: Philippians 1

Good morning! Today's challenge prompts introspection about any projects or aspirations initiated but left incomplete. I am talking about your goals on little pieces of paper or in the notebook buried under piles of stuff. Here's the thing: obstacles or waning motivation often halt progress, yet addressing these unfinished pursuits and rekindling confidence is vital. As you embark on this journey, let Philippians 1:6 be your guiding light: *"Being confident of this, that He who began a good work in you will carry it on to completion until the day of Christ Jesus."*

Here are Some Strategies for Tackling Unfinished Projects:

1. **List Unfinished Projects:** Jot down any incomplete endeavors, be they personal, professional, or creative. Perhaps a book you started, a fitness goal, a business concept, or any lingering aspiration.

2. **Reflect on Hurdles:** Contemplate why these projects remain incomplete. Identify specific challenges, internal struggles, or external factors that stalled progress. Understanding these barriers aids in effective resolution.

3. **Reconnect with Purpose:** Revisit the first vision driving these projects. Reflect on their significance, the impact envisioned, and why they matter. Rekindle your passion by reconnecting with these visions.

4. **Break it Down:** Overwhelming tasks often hinder progress. Divide each project into manageable steps or milestones. This approach fosters a sense of progress and momentum.

5. **Craft a Plan:** Develop an action plan for each unfinished project. Outline steps, set realistic deadlines, and distribute resources. A clear plan offers guidance toward completion.

6. **Seek Support:** Don't shy away from seeking encouragement from trusted confidants, family, or mentors. Share goals, seek guidance, and embrace their support for accountability and motivation.

7. **Celebrate Progress:** Acknowledge every stride toward completion. Recognize effort and progress made, fostering confidence and maintaining motivation.

Prayer: Dear God, I pray for the strength and strategies to finish what I have started and what needs my focus in this season of my life. Amen

Insight: Philippians 1:6 instills confidence that the good work commenced in you will reach fruition. Let this assurance embolden you to surmount obstacles, regain momentum, and triumph in completing these endeavors.

Date: _____

Reflection or Thoughts:

(Start writing your reflections, thoughts, prayers, or anything you wish to journal about in the space below.)

Day Four: The Power of Prayer and Confession

"Therefore confess your sins to each other and pray for each other so that you may be healed. The prayer of a righteous person is powerful and effective." (James 5:16, NIV)

Further Reading: James 5:16-18

Good morning! Today, let's delve into the profound impact of prayer and confession in the lives of believers. The scripture in James 5:16-18 highlights the potency of Elijah's prayer and confession, serving as a compelling example of the combined strength found in these spiritual practices. As we explore this, remember: Your most strategic position is found in the power of prayer!

Suggestions to Help You Augment Your Prayer Life:

1. **Confession's Significance:** Openly confessing sins fosters humility, vulnerability, and accountability within the Christian community. It paves the way for personal and relational healing and restoration.
2. **Power in Prayer:** James highlights prayer's incredible potency, rooted not in human strength but in our connection with God. A righteous person's prayers can yield miraculous results.
3. **Elijah's Example:** Elijah, though human and flawed, proved how fervent prayer evoked a three-and-a-half-year drought and its subsequent end, showcasing God's responsiveness.

Takeaway: James 5:16-18 underscores the importance of confession, the transformative might of prayer, and the exemplary faith of Elijah. May this passage inspire a vibrant prayer life, a pursuit of righteousness, and faith in God's responsiveness.

Seek Community: Join the 'Too Much to Gain to Lose' prayer community, born from an urgent call for a brother in need. Together, in a 30-day fasting and prayer journey, members witnessed miraculous breakthroughs and blessings. So can you. Visit www.cvwcoach.com/contact, follow the instructions, and send the message, 'I have too much to gain to lose.' Let's embark on a transformative journey of faith and unity, witnessing the power of prayer.

Prayer: Dear God, I pray my life produces fruit, and may your provisions rain down on my life. I confess my limitations and need of you.

Insight: Confession shows humility and further accountability to our Christian brethren. Through the power of prayer and confession, you can begin to break unacceptable habits.

Date: _____

Reflection or Thoughts:

(Start writing your reflections, thoughts, prayers, or anything you wish to journal about in the space below.)

Day Five: Prayer is Personal

"Let us then approach God's throne of grace with confidence, so that we may receive mercy and find grace to help us in our time of need." (Hebrews 4:16, NIV)

Further Reading: Hebrews 4

Good morning! Do you write down your thoughts? I have many journals that hold my private thoughts and prayers. Sometimes, I reread these thoughts and prayers when I face challenges to remind myself of the promises of God for my life and to remind myself of my answered prayers. Prayer is a staple in my life.

When was the last time you opened your heart and prayed to God? When did you last write down your thoughts and most earnest prayers?

Prayer is our direct line to God, a powerful tool connecting us to abundance. Consider approaching God in prayer to access His boundless resources and find the support you seek.

Take a moment. Speak your prayers aloud or quietly. Let's join in prayer with another person if you feel you need a little reinforcement. Seeking boldness and confidence to approach God's throne with reverence and gratitude is how you partner with God to get your prayers answered. Let's ask God for His abundant provision according to His riches in glory.

Prayer: Father, this morning, I boldly approach Your throne of grace, assured of finding mercy and help in my times of need. I'm grateful for the direct access prayer grants me. I come knowing Your loving kindness and readiness to help. Help me remember the significance of seeking Your guidance. I understand I don't face challenges alone but rely on Your mercy and grace for support. As I come to Your throne, grant me comfort, strength, and guidance through difficulties. In Jesus' name, I pray. Amen.

Insight: Hebrews 4:16 reminds us to approach God in prayer, confident of His readiness to extend grace and mercy, especially in our times of need.

Date: _____

Reflection or Thoughts:

(Start writing your reflections, thoughts, prayers, or anything you wish to journal about in the space below.)

Day Six: Worship with Joyful Hearts

"Worship the Lord with gladness; come before him with joyful songs." (Psalm 100:2, NIV)

Further Reading: Psalm 100:1-5

Good morning! Have you ever been overcome with joy? I am talking about the joy when you become free and untethered from your cares and concerns. A joyful heart ushers us into God's presence. Psalm 100:1-5 encourages joyful worship and gratitude to God, emphasizing serving Him with gladness, entering His presence with thanksgiving, and acknowledging His eternal goodness. Worship is your paid ticket to experience the fullness of God's joy.

On this particular day, joy filled my heart as I listened to "Let Praises Rise" by Miranda Curtis. The lyrics that resounded were, "Fill my heart till all they see is You, Lord." Worship brings our fullest attention to the Lord. May you experience the wonder of being in the presence of God.

Prayer: Dear God, thank you for the privilege to enter your presence to find joy, peace, and freedom. Whenever I feel burdened, invite me into your presence.

Insight: "It is done!" declares the Lord. Today, the heavens pour blessings upon those glorifying Him. Maintain joy, gladness, and gratitude for His deeds and forthcoming blessings.

Date: _____

Reflection or Thoughts:

(Start writing your reflections, thoughts, prayers, or anything you wish to journal about in the space below.)

Day Seven: Trusting God Fully

"Trust in the Lord with all your heart and lean not on your own understanding; in all your ways submit to him, and he will make your paths straight." (Proverbs 3:5-6, NIV)

Further Reading: Proverbs 3

Good morning! Take a moment to contemplate this verse. Consider its significance and how it applies to your life. Allow its wisdom to resonate within you. It emphasizes giving your whole heart, not just a part. Therefore, your reliance on God should be complete, without exception. As you reflect, assess the accuracy of your understanding regarding your situation or the journey you're undertaking.

Therefore, if you accept or recognize that God governs your life, you will not be inclined to depend on your thoughts, judgment, or understanding but on God to manage, lead, instruct, and guide you in a particular direction. This bible verse is one of the three pillar verses of my spiritual walk. I look to this verse daily for guidance, especially when uncertain about anything.

Reflective Questions:

1. What does it mean to you to trust the Lord wholeheartedly?

2. How often do you rely on your understanding instead of seeking God's guidance?

3. In what areas of your life do you need to submit to God and trust His direction?

4. Recall times when you trusted God. How did He guide your path?

Prayer: Dear God, I want to trust you fully. I place you at the helm of my plans because only your will for my life will prevail.

Insight: Pour out your heart in prayer to God. Express your desire to trust Him fully and seek His guidance in every aspect of life. Pray for strength and faith to surrender to His will.

Date: _____

Reflection or Thoughts:

(Start writing your reflections, thoughts, prayers, or anything you wish to journal about in the space below.)

_____
_____
_____
_____
_____
_____
_____
_____
_____
_____
_____
_____
_____
_____
_____
_____
_____
_____
_____
_____
_____
_____
_____

Day Eight: Embrace the New

"Forget the former things; do not dwell on the past."
(Isaiah 43:18, NIV)

Further Reading: Isaiah 43

Good morning! Today is the eighth day of your 42-day journey of prayer and fasting. The number 8 symbolizes a fresh start, representing God's work in bringing something new into your life. Embracing a fresh start is beneficial for everyone, and the start of a new year typically sets us on a path of embracing new opportunities.Imagine this scenario: You're entangled in life's circumstances, holding onto relationships or situations that no longer serve your purpose. Fear and uncertainty keep you from letting go. However, gentle nudges from God encourage you to release these grips and embrace something new. In moments of reflection, you realize that fighting against this process only brings exhaustion and frustration. Holding onto the past hinders progress.

With renewed faith, you surrender the old, embracing what God intends for you. Releasing these weights, you feel burdens lifted. Surrendering fears and doubts opens your heart to new possibilities. The journey isn't simple; there's a sense of loss or uncertainty. Yet, you trust God's good plans and embrace the change. In this surrender, you find peace and freedom. You notice God's work, unlocking new opportunities, relationships, and experiences. Closed doors begin to open, leading to growth and fulfillment.

This new path aligns with your passions and purpose, bringing joy and fulfillment. Challenges arise, but newfound strength and confidence guide you. You understand that you're exactly where you're meant to be. This journey teaches you the importance of letting go and embracing God's newness. Surrendering to His plan leads to transformation, guiding you closer to purpose, abundance, and fulfillment. **Are you up for an adventure of new experiences?**

Prayer: Dear God, I am ready to walk through the doors of surrender, forgiveness, and joy. May I treat every day as a new opportunity to fulfill your will.

Insight: Release past failures, disappointments, and regrets. Enjoy the present and focus on future possibilities. Releasing past failures doesn't erase our lessons but frees us from being defined by the past. God continually brings change, even in challenging situations. He provides in barren places, making a way where it seems impossible.

Day Eight: Embrace the New

"Forget the former things; do not dwell on the past."
(Isaiah 43:18, NIV)

Further Reading: Isaiah 43

Good morning! Today is the eighth day of your 42-day journey of prayer and fasting. The number 8 symbolizes a fresh start, representing God's work in bringing something new into your life. Embracing a fresh start is beneficial for everyone, and the start of a new year typically sets us on a path of embracing new opportunities.Imagine this scenario: You're entangled in life's circumstances, holding onto relationships or situations that no longer serve your purpose. Fear and uncertainty keep you from letting go. However, gentle nudges from God encourage you to release these grips and embrace something new. In moments of reflection, you realize that fighting against this process only brings exhaustion and frustration. Holding onto the past hinders progress.

With renewed faith, you surrender the old, embracing what God intends for you. Releasing these weights, you feel burdens lifted. Surrendering fears and doubts opens your heart to new possibilities. The journey isn't simple; there's a sense of loss or uncertainty. Yet, you trust God's good plans and embrace the change. In this surrender, you find peace and freedom. You notice God's work, unlocking new opportunities, relationships, and experiences. Closed doors begin to open, leading to growth and fulfillment.

This new path aligns with your passions and purpose, bringing joy and fulfillment. Challenges arise, but newfound strength and confidence guide you. You understand that you're exactly where you're meant to be. This journey teaches you the importance of letting go and embracing God's newness. Surrendering to His plan leads to transformation, guiding you closer to purpose, abundance, and fulfillment. **Are you up for an adventure of new experiences?**

Prayer: Dear God, I am ready to walk through the doors of surrender, forgiveness, and joy. May I treat every day as a new opportunity to fulfill your will.

Insight: Release past failures, disappointments, and regrets. Enjoy the present and focus on future possibilities. Releasing past failures doesn't erase our lessons but frees us from being defined by the past. God continually brings change, even in challenging situations. He provides in barren places, making a way where it seems impossible.

Date: _____

Reflection or Thoughts:

(Start writing your reflections, thoughts, prayers, or anything you wish to journal about in the space below.)

_____
_____
_____
_____
_____
_____
_____
_____
_____
_____
_____
_____
_____
_____
_____
_____
_____
_____
_____
_____
_____
_____
_____
_____
_____

Day Nine: God's Unconventional Provision

"The ravens brought him bread and meat in the morning and bread and meat in the evening, and he drank from the brook."
(1 Kings 17:6, NIV)

Further Reading: 1 Kings 17

Good morning! Are you facing impossible situations, financial struggles, or uncertainties? Are you in a metaphorical drought, feeling hopeless?

Consider how God miraculously sustained Elijah during a severe drought and famine. God used ravens– unclean birds to provide for Elijah, reminding us that our conventional thoughts or circumstances don't limit God's provision. If you are currently facing a situation where your human will dictate there's no way out, remember that Elijah was fed by an unlikely ally– the raven.

Prayer: Dear God, I pray for your provision through unconventional means today. May I find comfort in your limitless provision and assurance that you always work on my behalf. Lord, my shepherd, and provider, thank you for assuring me that I lack nothing.

Insight: God has a way of baffling the minds of those who look to him for divine support–the type of aid where we know nobody but God could have done it. Even in the most trying times, God will send provision and meet you at your point of need. For every God vision, there is God's provision.

Date: _____

Reflection or Thoughts:

(Start writing your reflections, thoughts, prayers, or anything you wish to journal about in the space below.)

_____
_____
_____
_____
_____
_____
_____
_____
_____
_____
_____
_____
_____
_____
_____
_____
_____
_____
_____
_____
_____
_____
_____
_____
_____

Day Ten: Seeking God's Insight

"Search me, God, and know my heart; test me and know my anxious thoughts. See if there is any offensive way in me, and lead me in the way everlasting." (Psalm 139:23-24, NIV)

Further Reading: Psalm 139

Good morning! Today, let's deepen our relationship with God through self-reflection and repentance.

King David showcases a posture of humility in Psalm 139. He invites God to examine his heart, thoughts, and actions, seeking guidance and correction. David desires God's complete knowledge of his innermost being, including thoughts and desires.

David confronts his anxious thoughts, demonstrating a willingness to confront fears, worries, and insecurities before God. He seeks guidance and comfort.

David also seeks correction for any offensive ways, desiring righteousness. Like David, let's invite God to search our hearts and actions, confronting fears and areas of sin. Surrender to God's examination and leading.

List five hindrances to your relationship with God and pray for His help to overcome them. (Space is provided on the next page).

Prayer: Dear God, I turn to you to quiet my anxiety, reveal my heart's hidden intentions, and help me confront my shortcomings.

Insight: Engaging in self-reflection and repentance can serve as a transformative tool in deepening our relationship with God, mirroring David's earnest desire for divine examination and guidance. It's a testament to the significance of being introspective, confronting anxieties, fears, and areas of sin before God, and allowing His wisdom and correction to lead us toward spiritual growth and righteousness.

Date: _____

Reflection or Thoughts:

(Start writing your reflections, thoughts, prayers, or anything you wish to journal about in the space below.)

Day Eleven: Embracing Today's Grace

"Therefore do not worry about tomorrow, for tomorrow will worry about itself. Each day has enough trouble of its own."
(Matthew 6:34, NIV)

Further Reading: Matthew 6

Good morning! As you ponder over this passage, remember the futility of worrying about tomorrow's needs. Place your complete trust in God, who knows and deeply cares for you.

Living in the present moment is vital. Each day carries its own challenges; worrying about the future distracts us from experiencing and trusting in God's present provision. Often, we miss today's blessings, worrying about tomorrow's uncertainties. This Scripture challenges our priorities, shifting our focus from material concerns to seeking God's kingdom and righteousness. Through this, we experience peace and assurance in God's provision, living in the sufficiency of His grace each day.

Gratitude Exercise:

Today, list five things you're grateful for:

1.

2.

3.

4.

5.

Prayer: Dear God, I remain content that you will send me daily provisions. Please help me to place my concerns and tomorrow in your hands.

Insight: Whatever your needs today, cast them upon God, knowing He understands and provides. Your prayers will be answered swiftly.

Date: _____

Reflection or Thoughts:

(Start writing your reflections, thoughts, prayers, or anything you wish to journal about in the space below.)

_____
_____
_____
_____
_____
_____
_____
_____
_____
_____
_____
_____
_____
_____
_____
_____
_____
_____
_____
_____
_____
_____
_____
_____

Day Twelve: Standing Firm in Faith

"Be alert and of sober mind. Your enemy the devil prowls around like a roaring lion looking for someone to devour."
(1 Peter 5:8, NIV)

Further Reading: 1 Peter 5

Good morning! Today, I pray for your strength and unwavering faith in God's grace. As believers, we are in an ongoing spiritual battle, needing to remain vigilant against the enemy's attacks.

In this passage, Peter compares the devil to a roaring lion, emphasizing the seriousness of our spiritual battle. It is akin to being relentlessly pursued by a fierce predator. Be vigilant! Stay awake and alert, become familiar with the enemy's tactics, and always be ready to resist.

Stand firm amidst your trials, knowing that God's promises form the bedrock of your resilience and victory. Understand that enduring struggles is common for believers. This realization brings comfort and solidarity, reminding you that you are part of a larger body of faith that supports and encourages one another.

Prayer: Dear God, empower me to stand in faith, knowing you will always protect me. Your presence is my greatest weapon. Grant me the gift of discernment to be aware and vigilant of the enemy's tactics.

Insight: Study how the lion hunts its prey. This will reveal the enemy's strategies for hunting you.

Date: _____

Reflection or Thoughts:

(Start writing your reflections, thoughts, prayers, or anything you wish to journal about in the space below.)

_____
_____
_____
_____
_____
_____
_____
_____
_____
_____
_____
_____
_____
_____
_____
_____
_____
_____
_____
_____
_____
_____
_____
_____

Day Thirteen: Healing From Betrayal

"My heart is in anguish within me; the terrors of death have fallen on me." (Psalm 55:4, NIV)

Further Reading: Psalm 55

Good morning! Have you grappled with the sting of betrayal from a colleague, friend, or loved one? Have you felt a lingering pain, even after the initial shock has waned? You're not alone. The psalmist in Psalm 55 poured out his distress before God, seeking solace amid betrayal and opposition. Like David, passionately call out to God, asking for His ear and finding refuge in Him. I have learned that betrayal can come from an unexpected person— a friend you thought you would grow old with, a business partner, a family member, or a spouse.

I have learned to acknowledge and process the hurt and to give no place to the spirit of offense. Those who betray us need the same grace we would want someone we have hurt to extend to us. Betrayal is ugly, but forgiving those who have betrayed us brings beauty to the experience.

Go ahead and think about the people who you believe have done something wrong to you. Seek God's help to release and forgive those who have wronged you. You can write your response in the reflection section provided.

Prayer: Dear God, heal me from the sting of betrayal and forgive those who have caused me pain. May I show them love and mercy and come to know that we are all deserving of forgiveness and grace.

Insight: Acknowledge the pain and seek healing to move towards victory. Release and forgive those who have hurt you. Experience the peace of God by seeking refuge in Him, transcending the scars of betrayal. Remember that forgiveness doesn't always equate to reconciliation.

Date: _____

Reflection or Thoughts:

(Start writing your reflections, thoughts, prayers, or anything you wish to journal about in the space below.)

_____
_____
_____
_____
_____
_____
_____
_____
_____
_____
_____
_____
_____
_____
_____
_____
_____
_____
_____
_____
_____
_____
_____
_____
_____

Day Fourteen: Praise For God's Provision

"The Lord is my strength and my shield; my heart trusts in him, and he helps me. My heart leaps for joy, and with my song, I praise him." (Psalm 28:7, NIV)

Further Reading: Psalm 28

Good morning! Today is for gratitude and praise. Reflect on this Scripture, believing God is your strength, shield, guide, and provider. Express what God means or is to you:

What God means to me:

[Write your personal encounter with God and what He represents to you in the space below.]

Date: _____

_____
_____
_____
_____
_____
_____
_____
_____
_____
_____
_____
_____
_____
_____

_____
_____
_____
_____
_____
_____
_____
_____
_____
_____
_____

Prayer: **[Write your prayer here].**
_____
_____
_____
_____
_____
_____

Insight: Acknowledge that your resources, strength, protection, and help come from God. This acknowledgment can make a world of difference when facing financial challenges or lack.

Day Fifteen: Embracing God's Plans

"For I know the plans I have for you," declares the Lord, "plans to prosper you and not to harm you, plans to give you hope and a future." (Jeremiah 29:11, NIV)

Further Reading: Jeremiah 29

Good morning! Someone shared with me how a shift in focus took her from feeling disheartened about her future and inability to land a job to having an unexpected door open for her. Imagine this was you. You recently graduated from college and are feeling disheartened about your future. Despite envisioning success in a specific career, job hunting yields no results, so you begin to grapple with discouragement and doubt your life choices.

In discovering Jeremiah 29:11, may you find solace. May you shift your focus, seeking God's guidance instead of dwelling on your plight. Understand that it is not God's will to create harm to you. But to give you peace, prosperity, and an expected or predetermined outcome. The promise that God has plans to prosper us is the type of hope we need to face our problems and challenges head-on. Through prayer and redirection, you can explore new paths and discover God's will for your life.

Are you in a season of uncertainty? Trust Jeremiah 29:11. Seek God's guidance, embrace new possibilities, and trust in His timing for a hopeful future aligned with His plans.

Prayer: Dear God, I know all too well that surrendering to your plans for my life is not easy, but I yield to your perfect plans for me.

Insight: Align your thoughts with God's plan to discover possibilities beyond your current circumstances. If you're feeling stuck or disheartened, examine your thoughts. What are you feeding your spirit? Redirect your focus toward the desired outcome.

Date: _____

Reflection or Thoughts:

(Start writing your reflections, thoughts, prayers, or anything you wish to journal about in the space below.)

_____
_____
_____
_____
_____
_____
_____
_____
_____
_____
_____
_____
_____
_____
_____
_____
_____
_____
_____
_____
_____
_____
_____

Day Sixteen: Trusting In God's Timing

"Wait for the Lord; be strong and take heart and wait for the Lord." (Psalm 27:14, NIV)

Further Reading: Psalm27

Good morning! Waiting is often seen as a burden in our fast-paced world, but God's Word offers a unique perspective. While life tempts us with instant results, Psalm 27:14 emphasizes the importance of patience in expecting the Lord's guidance.

Waiting is not idleness but an active period of growth. Your journey needs nurturing and patience, just as a seed takes time to germinate and grow into a tree. Waiting is the act of anticipating or expecting something to happen or a specific time to arrive. It involves patience and allowing time to pass without taking immediate action or making hasty decisions. Waiting can occur in various aspects of your life, such as opportunities, the right moment, or circumstances to align. While waiting may sometimes feel frustrating or unproductive, it serves a crucial purpose.

It allows you to gather more information, gain clarity, and ensure you are ready before taking action. Therefore, it is safe to say that waiting can be a form of protection. Use this waiting period to seek God's wisdom through prayer and guidance from mentors. Trust that God is orchestrating your life's journey– with each piece of the puzzle connection to the mosaic of your life experiences.

Prayer: Heavenly Father, grant me strength and patience as I wait. Guide me through this period, inspire my work, and let it bring glory to Your name. Amen.

Insight: You must embrace patience while waiting for God to move on your behalf. How can you embrace patience and trust during your waiting period? Write down any insights or action steps.

Date: _____

Reflection or Thoughts:

(Start writing your reflections, thoughts, prayers, or anything you wish to journal about in the space below.)

_____
_____
_____
_____
_____
_____
_____
_____
_____
_____
_____
_____
_____
_____
_____
_____
_____
_____
_____
_____
_____
_____
_____
_____
_____
_____
_____

Day Seventeen: Embracing God's Guidance

"I will instruct you and teach you in the way you should go; I will counsel you with my loving eye on you." (Psalm 32:8, NIV)

Further Reading: Psalm 32

Good morning! Two years ago, I embarked on an MBA program. This choice initially seemed unlikely, given my established career as a registered nurse. I felt frustrated and confused, yet cautiously hopeful. This unexpected turn challenged my 'self-designed' life plan. Starting a new course or journey without clear direction can be daunting and humbling. It demands acknowledging your lack of knowledge and adopting a learning mindset. In such situations, seeking guidance becomes crucial for navigating the journey successfully.

Psalm 32:8 assures us of God's intimate guidance in times of uncertainty. Surrendering to God's will requires humility and openness. It reminds you that you don't have to rely solely on your limited understanding or abilities. Instead, you can trust in a higher wisdom that surpasses your own.

Prayer: Heavenly Father, guide my steps and help me discern Your plans for my life. Lead me with Your wisdom and love. Amen.

Insight: Seek God's instruction through prayer and His Word. How can you surrender to God's guidance in your life? Write down any areas where you can let go and seek His instruction more deeply. Perhaps it is your relationship with money, career, business, or academics. Will you let God steward all your relationships?

Date: _____

Reflection or Thoughts:

(Start writing your reflections, thoughts, prayers, or anything you wish to journal about in the space below.)

Day Eighteen: Transforming Through Renewed Thinking

"Do not conform to the pattern of this world, but be transformed by the renewing of your mind. Then you will be able to test and approve what God's will is—his good, pleasing and perfect will."
(Romans 12:2, NIV)

Further Reading: Romans 12

Good morning! Romans 12:2 holds a powerful truth about walking closely with God by emphasizing the importance of renewing our minds. Our thoughts significantly impact our behaviors and life outcomes.

The world often pressures us to conform to its ideals, values, and trends, steering us away from God's truth, love, and righteousness. However, God calls us to a higher standard—a standard rooted in His Word.

We must actively renew our minds to cultivate a closer walk with God. This act means aligning our thoughts with God's Word, allowing His truth to shape our perspectives, decisions, and actions. Amidst a world focused on self and immediate gratification, God's Word guides us toward His perfect will.

Transforming our minds involves immersing ourselves in Scripture, meditating on God's promises, and seeking His wisdom. It requires consciously replacing worldly thinking with godly perspectives, filtering our thoughts through the lens of God's Word in every situation.

This process of renewing our minds demands discipline and intentionality. It necessitates dedicated prayer, Bible study, reflection, and surrounding ourselves with supportive believers who encourage our spiritual growth.

As we engage in this renewal, it goes beyond mere behavioral change. Our desires, motivations, and attitudes align with God's heart, leading to a closer walk with Him. We become more sensitive to His leading, discerning His will, and obeying His commands.

Through this transformation, we can discern and approve what aligns with God's will. Our understanding deepens concerning His purposes and plans for our lives. We become more attuned to His voice, receptive to His guidance, and willing to surrender our desires for His greater purposes.

Prayer: Heavenly Father, guide me in renewing my mind daily through Your Word and Holy Spirit. Transform my thoughts, attitudes, and behaviors to align with Your perfect will. Grant me discernment to recognize what is good, pleasing, and perfect according to Your plan. May my walk with You reflect Your love and grace. Amen.

Insight: Reflect on areas where your thoughts might align more with worldly views than God's Word. Consider intentionally renewing your mind and realigning your thoughts with His truth.

Date: _____

Reflection or Thoughts:

(Start writing your reflections, thoughts, prayers, or anything you wish to journal about in the space below.)

_____
_____
_____
_____
_____
_____
_____
_____
_____
_____
_____
_____
_____
_____
_____
_____
_____
_____
_____
_____
_____
_____
_____

Day Nineteen: Finding Peace Through Prayer and Gratitude

"And the peace of God, which transcends all understanding, will guard your hearts and your minds in Christ Jesus." (Philippians 4:7, NIV)

Further Reading: Philippians 4:6-7

Good morning! In our hectic lives, anxiety can easily overwhelm our hearts and minds. However, Philippians 4:6-7 provides a powerful strategy for finding peace amidst life's storms.

The passage urges us not to be anxious but to pray about everything. Talking to God through prayer lets us share our worries, fears, and needs, recognizing His authority over what we face.

Beyond prayer, the passage emphasizes approaching God with thanksgiving. Gratitude shifts our focus from worries to God's faithfulness and provision, opening our hearts to receive His peace.

To apply these strategies:

1. Identify your worries and bring them before God in prayer.
2. Present specific requests to God, sharing your fears and needs.
3. Cultivate gratitude daily, acknowledging God's blessings.
4. Surrender your anxieties to God, trusting His control.
5. Pray for God's peace to guard your heart and mind.

Consistently practicing prayer and gratitude helps us experience a shift in perspective, finding comfort in God's presence amidst life's challenges.

Prayer: Heavenly Father, I surrender my worries to You in moments of anxiety. Help me pray with specificity and gratitude, knowing You hear and answer. Fill me with Your surpassing peace, guarding my heart and mind in Christ Jesus. Amen.

Insight: Reflect on your current worries and anxieties. Consider specific steps to cultivate gratitude and surrender your concerns to God in prayer.

Date: _____

Reflection or Thoughts:

(Start writing your reflections, thoughts, prayers, or anything you wish to journal about in the space below.)

Day Twenty: Blessings in Obedience and Overcoming Financial Burdens

"The Lord will open the heavens, the storehouse of his bounty, to send rain on your land in season and to bless all the work of your hands. You will lend to many nations but will borrow from none."
(Deuteronomy 28:12, NIV)

Further Reading: Deuteronomy 28

Good morning! Which door do you hope will open for you? Is it a new job or an approval that will change your life for the good? Deuteronomy 28:12 underscores the blessings of obedience to God's commands. It promises God's provision and abundance to those who faithfully follow Him.

This verse highlights God's assurance to the Israelites of abundant blessings upon their land and work. It signifies that when we align our efforts with God's will and steward our resources wisely, He blesses us and allows us to bless others.

However, this verse doesn't guarantee only material wealth. God's blessings encompass spiritual, emotional, and relational growth. Walking in obedience invites His blessings into every facet of our lives.

To achieve financial freedom:

1. Take a finance class. There are tons of free information available on YouTube. Choose one from a credible source.

2. Create and stick to a budget, prioritizing debt repayment.

3. Cultivate contentment and avoid unnecessary spending.

4. Seek counsel and financial education for guidance.

5. Explore ways to increase income while reducing unnecessary expenses. How about monetizing a couple of things you are naturally good at?

6. Surrender financial burdens to God and trust in His provision.

You'll progress toward financial freedom through discipline, consistency, and obedience aligned with God's will, trusting in His faithfulness.

Prayer: Heavenly Father, guide me to overcome financial burdens and live obediently to Your will. Grant me wisdom to manage resources and discipline to steward them well. Help me find contentment and trust in Your provision. Amen.

Insight: Consider which strategies resonate most with your financial situation. Jot down practical steps to implement these strategies in your life, seeking God's guidance throughout the journey. The Lord told me, "Your money flows to where your values and attention reside. To understand where your money goes, assess where your time and attention are invested."

Date: _____

Reflection or Thoughts:

(Start writing your reflections, thoughts, prayers, or anything you wish to journal about in the space below.)

_____
_____
_____
_____
_____
_____
_____
_____
_____
_____
_____
_____
_____
_____
_____
_____
_____
_____
_____
_____
_____
_____
_____

Day Twenty-One: Seeking Refuge in God's Protection

"I will say of the Lord, 'He is my refuge and my fortress, my God, in whom I trust." (Psalm 91:2, NIV)

Further Reading: Psalm 91

Good morning! Prayer has always been my guide into God's refuge. This haven, synonymous with His protection, brings peace and joy regardless of my circumstances. Accessing God's refuge is as simple as asking, expressing gratitude, and praising Him.

Here's a prayer seeking God's refuge and protection:

Almighty Father, with a heart full of gratitude and reverence, I recognize Your unwavering sovereignty and faithfulness. Grant me Your presence and wisdom.

Lord, Psalm 91:1 assures me, "Whoever dwells in the shelter of the Most High will rest in the shadow of the Almighty." I earnestly desire to reside in Your presence, finding refuge and solace in Your loving embrace. Guide me to dwell in You, seeking shelter and protection in every aspect of my life.

Verse 2 declares You as my fortress, my refuge in times of trouble. Today, I surrender my fears, trusting in Your unyielding protection as my ultimate source of security. Though daily battles surround me, Your promises shine in adversity, and Your faithfulness becomes my shield.

I find comfort in knowing You stand by me in every trial, assuring my deliverance from harm. Your Word promises that no evil shall befall me, and no plague shall come near my dwelling. I cling to this promise, especially in times of uncertainty.

Today, I pray for Your divine protection over my life. Shield me from all harm, whether visible or hidden, known or unknown. Grant me wisdom to make choices aligned with Your will.

Father, verse fourteen assures Your promise to rescue those who love You. I declare my love for You and seek deliverance from trials and temptations. Strengthen my faith to walk in obedience and experience Your mighty hand at work.

Lord, I embrace the profound promises in verses 15-16. You declare that when I call upon You, You will answer. You promise to be with me in times of trouble, to deliver and honor me. I thank You for Your unfailing faithfulness and the assurance of satisfaction with a long life, revealing Your salvation.

As I conclude this prayer, grant me the grace to live out the truths in Psalm 91. Help me dwell in Your presence, trust in Your protection, and walk obediently in Your will. May Your promises continually empower, shield, and uplift me. In the precious name of Jesus, I pray. Amen.

Insight: Rest assured that you are safe in God's will.

Date: _____

Reflection or Thoughts:

(Start writing your reflections, thoughts, prayers, or anything you wish to journal about in the space below.)

Day Twenty-Two: Finding Strength in Trust

"The Lord is my light and my salvation—whom shall I fear? The Lord is the stronghold of my life—of whom shall I be afraid?"
(Psalm 27:1, NIV)

Further Reading: Psalm 27:1-14

Good morning! In Psalm 27, David lays bare his heart before the Lord, showcasing unwavering trust and confidence in God's faithfulness. This Psalm serves as a profound reminder that even during trials, we find strength and courage in the Lord.

Let's glean inspiration from David's words. Verse 1 begins with a resounding declaration of trust: "The Lord is my light and my salvation—whom shall I fear?" David acknowledges the Lord as his ultimate source of strength and deliverance.

As believers, we find comfort in knowing God is our light, guiding us through darkness and salvation, rescuing us from every trouble. With the Lord as our stronghold, earthly threats and challenges lose their power to evoke fear.

In verses 4-6, David expresses his longing to dwell in the Lord's house and continually seek His presence. He yearns to behold the beauty of the Lord and take refuge in His sanctuary. This Psalm reveals David's deep intimacy with God and his understanding that true strength and courage are found in the presence of the Almighty. When we cultivate a similar yearning for God's presence, we experience His peace and find renewed strength to face any situation.

David's unwavering trust in the Lord echoes in verses 7-10. Despite adversaries, he remains confident that God will never forsake him. Even if his earthly family were to abandon him, David trusts that the Lord would never leave nor forsake him. This assurance encourages us to place our confidence in God, knowing He will never abandon us.

In the final verses, David encourages us to wait patiently for the Lord, to be strong and take heart. God is our ultimate source of strength and will deliver us in His perfect timing. David's life experiences bear witness to God's faithfulness, confirming the goodness and trustworthiness of the Lord.

Reflecting on Psalm 27:1-14, let David's unwavering trust inspire us in God's faithfulness. In times of darkness, fear, and uncertainty, may we find strength and courage in the Lord—our light and salvation. Continually seeking His presence, let us trust He will guide us and provide refuge. May we patiently await His deliverance, assured He fights alongside us.

Prayer: Dear Heavenly Father, I thank You for Psalm 27, a beautiful reminder of Your faithfulness and the strength we discover in You. Help me trust You wholeheartedly as my light and salvation. May I continually seek Your presence and refuge, granting me patience as I await Your deliverance. Infuse me with strength and courage to confront every challenge in Your name. Amen.

Insight: Reflect on areas where you need strength and courage in the Lord. Take a moment to seek His presence and guidance, knowing He is your ultimate source of strength and deliverance.

Date: _____

Reflection or Thoughts:

(Start writing your reflections, thoughts, prayers, or anything you wish to journal about in the space below.)

_____
_____
_____
_____
_____
_____
_____
_____
_____
_____
_____
_____
_____
_____
_____
_____
_____
_____
_____
_____
_____
_____

Day Twenty-Three: Embracing God's Intimate Knowledge

"You have searched me, Lord, and you know me."
(Psalm 139:1, NIV)

Further Reading: Psalm 139:1-6

Good morning! It is one thing to know God but another to be known by him. Read it twice. Psalm 139 reveals King David's deep reverence for God's intimate knowledge and unconditional love. In these verses, David marvels at God's profound understanding and presence in his life.

Let's delve into this passage, drawing inspiration from David's words. Verse 1 opens with a profound acknowledgment: "You have searched me, Lord, and you know me." David acknowledges God's complete knowledge of his innermost being. This recognition of God's omniscience and intimate understanding of every aspect of our lives should bring comfort and assurance. It means we are never alone and can trust God's perfect knowledge and guidance.

In verses 2-3, David marvels at God's knowledge of his actions and thoughts. He acknowledges God's awareness of his daily activities and understands his motives and intentions. This realization prompts David to embrace God's presence and seek His guidance in every aspect of his life. Similarly, we can find peace knowing that God is intimately acquainted with our lives, trusting Him to guide us on the right path.

Continuing in verses 4-6, David expresses awe at God's all-encompassing knowledge. He acknowledges that God knows it completely even before a word is on his tongue. This recognition of God's omniscience should lead us to approach Him with reverence and honesty, knowing He already knows our deepest thoughts and desires. We can find comfort in the fact that God understands us better than we understand ourselves.

Prayer: Heavenly Father, I stand in awe of Your intimate knowledge and boundless love. Help me to fully embrace the truth that You know me completely and understand me better than I understand myself. May I find solace in Your presence and seek Your guidance in every aspect of my life. Teach me to approach You with honesty and surrender, trusting that You will lead me on the right path. In Jesus' name, I pray. Amen.

Insight: Reflect on the depth of God's knowledge and love for you. How does knowing that He understands your thoughts, motives, and desires make you feel? Consider how you can embrace His presence and seek His guidance daily. Trust in His perfect knowledge and unconditional love as you surrender to His leading.

Date: _____

Reflection or Thoughts:

(Start writing your reflections, thoughts, prayers, or anything you wish to journal about in the space below.)

Day Twenty-Four: Encountering God's Presence

"Now Moses used to take a tent and pitch it outside the camp some distance away, calling it the 'tent of meeting.' Anyone inquiring of the Lord would go to the tent of meeting outside the camp."(Exodus 33:7, NIV)

Further Reading: Exodus 33:7-10

Good morning! Let's explore this passage for insights that can enrich our spiritual walk.

Here's a scripture that narrates Moses' ritual of setting up a tent outside the camp, called the "tent of meeting." This sacred place signified communion with God. When Moses entered, the pillar of cloud, representing God's presence, descended—a visible reminder of God's guidance and presence.

The story continues as Moses entered; the people stood in awe at the entrance of their tents, reverently worshiping while Moses communed with God. This act showcased their recognition of God's authority and their desire to be close to Him.

What a show of the profound relationship between God and Moses—God spoke to Moses face to face as one speaks to a friend. This exceptional connection set Moses apart as a chosen leader and mediator for the Israelites.

This passage reveals vital aspects of our relationship with God. It emphasizes seeking His presence, trusting His guidance, and approaching Him reverently. Like Moses, we can create dedicated spaces in our lives—moments of prayer and worship—seeking communion with God, similar to what we do through this devotional.

The descending cloud signifies God's perpetual presence and guidance throughout life's journey. It reassures us that He leads and shields us.

The Israelites' response teaches us to approach God with awe and humility, recognizing His holiness and sovereignty and seeking His will.

Lastly, the intimacy between God and Moses shows the possibility of a personal relationship with our Creator through Jesus Christ. Knowing He hears and responds, we can speak openly, honestly, and intimately.

Prayer: Gracious God, lead me to seek Your presence earnestly. Help me create sacred spaces for communion with You. Grant me the humility to approach You in reverence, recognizing Your sovereignty. May my heart be open to a deeper, more intimate relationship with You. In Jesus' name, amen.

Insight: Reflect on how you seek God's presence in your life. Are there dedicated moments or spaces where you commune with Him? How might you deepen this communion and approach Him with greater reverence and openness?

Let us embrace the lessons from this passage—seeking God's presence, trusting His guidance, and nurturing a close relationship with our Creator.

Date: _____

Reflection or Thoughts:

(Start writing your reflections, thoughts, prayers, or anything you wish to journal about in the space below.)

_____
_____
_____
_____
_____
_____
_____
_____
_____
_____
_____
_____
_____
_____
_____
_____
_____
_____
_____
_____
_____
_____
_____

Day Twenty-Five: Rahab's Faith and Strategies for Success

"I know that the Lord has given you this land and that a great fear of you has fallen on us, so that all who live in this country are melting in fear because of you." (Joshua 2:10, NIV)

Further Reading: Joshua 2

Good morning! Imagine this: Joshua's spies sneaking into Jericho, scoping out the Promised Land. Guess where they find shelter? Rahab's house. This was an unexpected encounter with faith! It is good when even your enemies recognize what your God can do.

In verse 10, Rahab recounts how the news of God's miraculous deeds affected Jericho, underscoring the impact of Israel's testimonies and God's reputation on surrounding nations.

This passage teaches vital lessons: the influence of God's mighty acts and His people's testimony on others. Rahab's response proves how witnessing God's works can ignite faith in others' hearts. Moreover, her acknowledgment expands God's sovereignty beyond Israel's borders.

Rahab's faith challenges us to recognize God's authority and sovereignty. Her story also foreshadows God's redemptive work as Rahab, despite her occupation, becomes part of Jesus Christ's lineage (Matthew 1:5).

Her story emphasizes God's grace for all who trust Him, regardless of their past or background. Reflecting on Rahab's faith, we're encouraged to share God's testimonies, knowing they can lead others to faith in Christ.

Rahab's Strategies for Success:

1. Recognize Opportunities in Unconventional Circumstances: Rahab's story teaches the importance of seizing unexpected opportunities. Despite her circumstances, she recognized a chance to help the Israelite spies, knowing it could change her destiny. Similarly, being perceptive in unconventional situations can lead to impactful opportunities.

2. Confront and Evaluate Fears: Rahab faced fears but didn't let them hinder her. Instead, she assessed potential outcomes before acting. Similarly, confronting fears and evaluating their consequences empowers better decision-making.

3. Create Actionable Plans: Rahab's success lies in her actionable plan to protect the spies and her family. Breaking down actions into clear steps ensures effective execution. In life, outlining clear, actionable steps is key to achieving goals.

4. Embrace Authenticity and Uniqueness: The scarlet cord Rahab used became a symbol of her identity and safety. It set her apart. Similarly, embracing authenticity and uniqueness allows for individual contributions and success. Being true to oneself can make a lasting impact.

Prayer: Dear God, I know that divine wisdom comes through you. Teach me your ways and help me to pursue my goal with courage and authenticity.

Insight: Rahab's story in Joshua 2:9-11 provides strategies for navigating challenges and seizing opportunities. Being perceptive, confronting fears, planning effectively, and embracing authenticity can lead to success. May Rahab's boldness and authenticity inspire you to pursue your goals with courage and authenticity.

Date: _____

Reflection or Thoughts:

(Start writing your reflections, thoughts, prayers, or anything you wish to journal about in the space below.)

Day Twenty-Six: God's Promise of Guidance and Hidden Treasures

"I will go before you and will level the mountains; I will break down gates of bronze and cut through bars of iron."
(Isaiah 45:2, NIV)

Further Reading: Isaiah 45

Good morning! Isaiah 45:2 vividly illustrates God's commitment to clearing our paths and providing abundant blessings. The imagery of making crooked places straight and breaking formidable barriers signifies God's power over seemingly insurmountable challenges.

Just as a skilled excavator removes obstacles and clears the land before construction begins, God promises to pave a clear path for us. This assurance reminds us that despite obstacles, nothing is impossible for Him. We can lean on His strength and guidance, confident that He will always chart a course for us.

In verse three, God pledges, "I will grant you treasures concealed in darkness, riches hidden in secret places, so that you may know that I am the Lord, the God of Israel, who calls you by name." Here, God's promise of hidden treasures extends beyond material wealth. It encompasses spiritual blessings, divine wisdom, and provisions beyond our understanding.

These blessings aren't solely for our benefit; they reveal God's character and faithfulness. He desires us to acknowledge Him as our Lord, the intimate God who knows us individually and beckons us by name. His provisions and guidance in our lives are testimonies to His sovereignty and boundless love.

Reflecting on Isaiah 45:2-3 invites us to find solace in God's promises. He goes ahead, clearing hurdles and making a way. His promise of hidden treasures transcends material wealth, encompassing divine blessings. May we place our trust in His guidance and provision, recognizing Him as our intimately knowing Lord.

Prayer: Gracious Father, I'm grateful for Your promises of guidance and provision. Strengthen my trust in Your wisdom and guidance. Help me recognize the hidden blessings You provide and reveal Your faithfulness in my life. Instill in me an unwavering reliance on Your provision and direction in every facet of my journey. In Jesus' name, Amen.

Insight: Consider the promises in Isaiah 45:2-3. How does it feel knowing God goes ahead, smoothing out our obstacles? Reflect on the hidden treasures He's provided in your life. How might you deepen your trust in His guidance and provision? Let His assurances bring comfort and certainty as you navigate life's journey.

Date: _____

Reflection or Thoughts:

(Start writing your reflections, thoughts, prayers, or anything you wish to journal about in the space below.)

Day Twenty-Seven: Embracing Unity and Diversity

"Now if the foot should say, 'Because I am not a hand, I do not belong to the body,' it would not for that reason stop being part of the body." (1 Corinthians 12:15, NIV)

Further Reading: 1 Corinthians 12:14-21

Good morning! We are each a part of the whole—each part working in unison with the other. Think of the church as a team. We're all different but work together, just like parts of a body. Each person has a special role and gifts from God.

Paul says comparing ourselves to others in the church is not good. Every person is important, no matter what they do. Also, don't undervalue your role! What you do matters.

When we think about 1 Corinthians 12:14-21, we understand that we're all unique and needed in the church. Everyone's gift and role matter; we strengthen the team when we embrace and support each other. That's how we show God's love to the world.

Here are three tips to help you embrace unity and diversity:

1. Make sure everyone feels seen and appreciated for what they bring to the table. Listen actively, talk openly, and create an atmosphere where everyone's ideas are respected.

2. Help people figure out what they're good at and passionate about. Understanding their unique abilities allows them to see better how they fit into the bigger picture.

3. Celebrate and learn from our diverse backgrounds and viewpoints. Each person's unique gifts and roles are vital for

the team's success. Let's value and understand each other better.

Prayer: Dear God, help me value the people in my life. May I applaud and celebrate who they are to me and their uniqueness. I pray I am humble enough to know there is still so much I can learn from others.

Insight: These strategies create a harmonious environment where individuals leverage their unique gifts and functions for the collective good. Just as the body runs smoothly, each part fulfilling its role, a group that embraces individual strengths and purposes achieves exceptional results.

Date: _____

Reflection or Thoughts:

(Start writing your reflections, thoughts, prayers, or anything you wish to journal about in the space below.)

_____
_____
_____
_____
_____
_____
_____
_____
_____
_____
_____
_____
_____
_____
_____
_____
_____
_____
_____
_____
_____
_____
_____
_____

Day Twenty-Eight: Sacrificial Love in Action

"This is how we know what love is: Jesus Christ laid down his life for us. And we ought to lay down our lives for our brothers and sisters." (1 John 3:16, NIV)

Further Reading: 1 John 3:16-18

Good morning! Let's talk about the incredible power of sacrificial love. Picture this: someone laying down their life for others—a profound act that showcases deep, genuine love. Inspired by this, we're encouraged to selflessly extend love and serve others.

Now, it's not just about talking the talk. There's a reminder to back up words with actions, emphasizing the need for tangible expressions of empathy, especially when it comes to meeting others' needs.

Reflecting on 1 John 3:16-18 inspires us to embody Christ's sacrificial love. His love should compel us to selflessly care for others, meeting their needs with compassion and empathy. It encourages us not to be content with mere expressions but to actively demonstrate love through genuine acts of kindness. By doing so, we emulate Christ's transformative love to a world in need.

Prayer: Gracious Father, I thank You for Christ's sacrificial love, a profound example for me. Help me grasp the depth of Your love and empower me to care for others selflessly. Open my eyes to the needs around me and instill genuine compassion and empathy in me. May my love be rooted in truth, reflecting Your immense love for me. In Jesus' name, Amen.

Insight: How does Christ's sacrificial love inspire you to love others? Contemplate practical ways to show love through actions and truth. How can you extend compassion and care to those in need?

Allow Christ's love to motivate impactful actions, reflecting His transformative love to others.

Date: _____

Reflection or Thoughts:

(Start writing your reflections, thoughts, prayers, or anything you wish to journal about in the space below.)

Day Twenty-Nine: Finding Peace Amidst Challenges

"I have told you these things, so that in me you may have peace. In this world, you will have trouble. But take heart! I have overcome the world." (John 16:33, NIV)

Further Reading: John 16

Good morning! John 16:33 offers profound comfort and encouragement in the face of life's trials. In this verse, Jesus prepares His disciples for His impending departure and the difficulties they will encounter. Acknowledging the inevitability of tribulation in this world, Jesus reassures them of His presence and the peace found in Him.

Jesus doesn't conceal the challenges ahead; He acknowledges the reality of trials. This acknowledgment doesn't exempt us from life's struggles but reminds us of our shared human experience. Despite these challenges, Jesus offers solace by being the source of genuine peace.

Moreover, Jesus declares His victory over the world. Through His life, death, and resurrection, He triumphed over the very struggles that bring turmoil into our lives. As His followers, we find hope and strength in His triumph.

This verse doesn't promise exemption from difficulties but assures us of peace and victory in Christ. We find the resilience and confidence to face life's trials through faith in Him. Our struggles do not define us, for we are anchored in the overcoming power of Christ.

Prayer: Dear God, thank you for your wonderful peace as I walk through my challenges. May I feel the comfort and peace of knowing you.

Insight: Reflecting on John 16:33, we find solace in Christ's promise of peace and victory. We draw strength and hope in Him, navigating life's challenges with unwavering faith.

Date: _____

Reflection or Thoughts:

(Start writing your reflections, thoughts, prayers, or anything you wish to journal about in the space below.)

Day Thirty: Surrendering Plans to God's Will

"Commit to the Lord whatever you do, and he will establish your plans." (Proverbs 16:3, NIV)

Further Reading: Proverbs 16

Good morning! Ever felt like you've got a ton of plans and goals, but there's this nudge to surrender it all to the Lord? Proverbs 16:3 is all about that—it's like the guide to finding real success and fulfillment by syncing up your dreams with God's game plan. You can make that happen today!

Here's How You Can Submit to God's Will:

1. **Seek God's Guidance:** Start every plan by seeking God's wisdom through prayer and meditation. Invite His presence into your decision-making process.

2. **Surrender Plans to God:** Release attachment to personal desires and submit to God's divine will. Trust His wisdom over your own, acknowledging His perfect plans.

3. **Align with God's Word:** Let God's Word guide your plans. Ensure they reflect His values and principles, becoming a foundation for your aspirations.

4. **Remain Open to Redirection:** Be receptive to God's redirection, understanding His plans may differ from yours. Be willing to adjust plans according to His guidance.

5. **Trust in God's Faithfulness:** Lean on God's promises and faithfulness throughout your journey. Trust that He's working for your good even in setbacks.

6. **Embrace Patience and Perseverance:** Be patient; God's timing may differ from yours. Trust His perfect timing and endure with patience.

As we meditate on Proverbs 16:3, let's commit our plans to God, seeking His guidance and aligning our aspirations with His will. Trust in His faithfulness, remain open to His redirection and embrace patience. May our plans reflect His wisdom and bring glory to His name.

Prayer: Heavenly Father, I surrender my plans to You today. Guide me in aligning my aspirations with Your will. Grant me patience and trust in Your faithfulness. May my plans honor You and bring glory to Your name. In Jesus' name, Amen.

Insight: Consider applying the strategies from Proverbs 16:3 to align your plans with God's will. Reflect on any necessary adjustments or surrendering you need to make. Spend time in prayer, committing your plans to God, and trusting in His guidance.

Date: _____

Reflection or Thoughts:

(Start writing your reflections, thoughts, prayers, or anything you wish to journal about in the space below.)

_____
_____
_____
_____
_____
_____
_____
_____
_____
_____
_____
_____
_____
_____
_____
_____
_____
_____
_____
_____
_____
_____
_____
_____
_____

Day Thirty-One: Embracing a Season of Power and Prosperity

"That person is like a tree planted by streams of water, which yields its fruit in season and whose leaf does not wither— whatever they do prospers." (Psalm 1:3, NIV)

Further Reading: Psalm 1:1-3

Good morning! Imagine, if you will, that everything you do prospers. Picture yourself as a tree with roots growing down to the water, bearing fruit in season, and your leaves never withering. This is the image of a person who delights in God's law, symbolizing a new season filled with strength and success. Today, let's delve into this passage and explore ways to identify and embrace this new phase in our lives.

The Psalm starts by emphasizing our associations and choices. It states, "Blessed is the one who doesn't follow the advice of the wicked, stand around with sinners, or hang out with scoffers." This verse urges us to be conscious of our company and influences. We must distance ourselves from negativity to enter this new season and align with those who walk in righteousness.

Shifting the focus to delight and meditation on God's law, it reads, "But they delight in the Lord's instruction, and they meditate on it day and night." Finding joy in studying and applying God's Word is key. Through this delight and reflection, we gain wisdom and Insight into His ways.

Delighting in God's law is compared to a tree planted by streams of water, signifying stability, nourishment, and productivity. It signifies a season of strength and success. Just as a tree flourishes when well-nourished, we thrive by immersing ourselves in God's Word and aligning our lives with His principles.

In this new season of power and prosperity, the Psalm assures that our endeavors will prosper– not necessarily material wealth, but a spiritual richness bringing fulfillment, peace, and purpose. Aligning with God's Word brings favor and blessings in all facets of life.

To recognize and embrace this new season, prioritize your relationship with God and His Word. Cultivate a love for studying and meditating on His law. This immersion gives clarity and direction for a transformative season of power and prosperity.

Commit to delighting in the law of the Lord, meditating on it day and night. As you do, become like trees planted by streams of water, flourishing and bearing fruit in every season. Experience the blessings that come from aligning your life with His Word.

Prayer: Heavenly Father, I desire to diligently delight in Your law and meditate on it. Help me prioritize my relationship with You and Your Word. Open my heart and mind to receive Your wisdom and guidance. Guide me to identify and embrace this new season of power and prosperity that arises from aligning my life with Your principles. May I flourish like a tree planted by streams of water. In Jesus' name, I pray. Amen.

Insight: Reflect on Psalm 1:1-3. How can you delight in God's law and meditate on it consistently? Are there adjustments needed in your life to align with God's Word? Spend time in prayer, seeking God's guidance as you embark on this new season.

Date: _____

Reflection or Thoughts:

(Start writing your reflections, thoughts, prayers, or anything you wish to journal about in the space below.)

Day Thirty-Two: God's Protection and Victory

"No weapon forged against you will prevail, and you will refute every tongue that accuses you. This is the heritage of the servants of the Lord, and this is their vindication from me," declares the Lord." (Isaiah 54:17, NIV)

Further Reading: Isaiah 54

Good morning! Isaiah 54:17 promises God's protection and triumph over adversities. Let's delve into this verse and ponder its assurance in our lives.

"No weapon formed against you shall prosper, and you shall refute every tongue that rises against you in judgment. This is the heritage of the servants of the Lord, and their vindication from me," says the Lord.

This promise assures the servants of the Lord protection and vindication directly from God Himself. **Here's how I apply this scripture to my life:**

1. **Protection from every weapon:** God assures that no physical or spiritual weapon formed against us will prevail. He is our ultimate protector, shielding us from harm and ensuring our safety. In challenges, His intervention renders weapons against us powerless.

2. **Refuting accusations:** God promises that accusations and condemnations will not stand against us. He defends our character and reputation as we walk in righteousness and obedience. God silences those seeking to harm us unjustly.

3. **Heritage of God's servants:** This promise is exclusive to all serving the Lord. We inherit His divine protection and

vindication as His chosen people, a privilege signifying His covenant promises.

4. **Vindication from the Lord:** God declares this promise, assuring our victory and standing as our advocate. Trusting His faithfulness, we find comfort in His protection and courage in His vindication.

As we contemplate Isaiah 54:17, find strength and reassurance in this promise. Regardless of challenges, God is our protector and defender. No weapon formed against us will prevail, and every accusation against us will fail. This assurance is not based on our strength but God's unwavering faithfulness to His servants.

Hold this promise in times of hardship, knowing God is with us. Find comfort in His protection, courage in His vindication, and peace in His presence. Walk confidently, trusting in the unfailing promises of Isaiah 54:17, experiencing God's victorious power in your life.

Prayer: Heavenly Father, thank You for the promise of protection and vindication. I trust Your faithfulness and love for Your servants. Strengthen me to walk in righteousness, knowing You are my ultimate protector. Help me refute every accusation and find comfort in Your presence. May Your promises be my hope in every season. In Jesus' name, Amen.

Insight: In my own life, I have seen time and time again that there are blessings in God's protection – even the plans that did not work out. Reflect on Isaiah 54:17. How does this promise speak to your circumstances? Are there areas where you need to trust in God's faithfulness and seek His protection? Spend time in prayer, surrendering your concerns to God, and trusting in His unwavering promises.

Date: _____

Reflection or Thoughts:

(Start writing your reflections, thoughts, prayers, or anything you wish to journal about in the space below.)

_____
_____
_____
_____
_____
_____
_____
_____
_____
_____
_____
_____
_____
_____
_____
_____
_____
_____
_____
_____
_____
_____
_____
_____
_____
_____

Day Thirty-Three: Embracing Faith Through Hearing

"Consequently, faith comes from hearing the message, and the message is heard through the word about Christ."
(Romans 10:17, NIV)

Further Reading: Romans 10

Good morning! Romans 10:17 is your GPS to faith. You know, like deciding whether to turn left or right? Faith is crafted through the power of hearing the word of Christ. Without the word of God, there's no faith for the believer. Let's unpack this and consider how tuning into God's words can fuel our faith journey. Ready to dive in together?

What Faith is:

1. **The Source of Faith:** Faith isn't an outcome of human endeavor; it's a divine gift from God. Through His grace, we're granted the capacity to believe and trust in Him. Our faith originates from encountering the message of Christ, the gospel of salvation and reconciliation with God. When received with an open heart, this message can transform lives and ignite faith within us.

2. **Attentiveness to the Message:** We must actively listen to Christ's message. Listening goes beyond just hearing—it means actively engaging with and understanding the truths in God's Word. This includes studying Scripture, tuning into sermons, participating in Bible studies, and seeking opportunities to gain experience in our understanding of Christ. Immersing ourselves in God's Word strengthens our faith, helping us discern His voice more clearly.

3. **The Word about Christ:** The message that kindles faith is centered on Christ—His life, teachings, sacrificial death, and glorious resurrection. It reveals His redemptive work and the hope He offers. The Word about Christ forms the basis of our faith, unveiling God's love, grace, and plan of salvation. Through this message, we encounter Jesus and experience the transformative power of His presence.

As we reflect on Romans 10:17, let's appreciate the role of attentive listening in our faith journey. Faith isn't static; it's a dynamic relationship with God nurtured through actively receiving and internalizing His Word. Through this process, our hearts, minds, and spirits transform.

Let's prioritize actively engaging with the message of Christ—immersing ourselves in His Word and seeking opportunities to learn and grow. Our faith will be fortified as we do so, and we'll encounter the depth of God's love and grace.

Prayer: Heavenly Father, I thank You for the precious gift of faith. Help me to listen and receive Your Word with an open heart continually. Nurture within me a hunger for Your truth and a desire to deepen my understanding of Christ. Strengthen my faith as I immerse myself in Your Word and seek opportunities for spiritual growth. May my faith be deeply rooted in the message of Christ, transforming every sphere of my life. In Jesus' name, Amen.

Insight: Reflect on Romans 10:17. How has encountering Christ's message impacted your faith journey? Are there areas in your life where you need to prioritize attentive listening and engage more deeply with God's Word?

Take a moment in prayer, seeking God's guidance and asking for a deeper hunger for His truth and a strengthened faith through actively listening and receiving His Word.

Date: _____

Reflection or Thoughts:

(Start writing your reflections, thoughts, prayers, or anything you wish to journal about in the space below.)

Day Thirty-Four: The Power of Faith and Prayer

"Truly I tell you, if anyone says to this mountain, 'Go, throw yourself into the sea,' and does not doubt in their heart but believes that what they say will happen, it will be done for them. Therefore I tell you, whatever you ask for in prayer, believe that you have received it, and it will be yours." (Mark 11:23-24, NIV)

Further Reading: Mark 11

Good morning! Imagine a faith where you tell a mountain to throw itself into the sea, and it happens. This is the promise of Mark 11:23-24—the transformative potential of faith and prayer. Now, think about your life. What "mountains" do you face? What if you could tackle them head-on with that kind of faith? Jesus is saying when you pray, really believe it has already happened, and it's yours! This is how we approach challenges. So, what mountain are you thinking of throwing into the sea with your faith today? As you reflect on the challenges or obstacles in your life, consider the following:

1. **The Power of Faith:** Jesus highlights the incredible power of faith. Using the imagery of speaking to a mountain—a symbol of a **huge** obstacle or challenge—He demonstrates the authority faith bestows upon believers. We can command obstacles to be removed with unwavering faith, free from doubt. Faith enables us to tap into God's supernatural power, witnessing miraculous breakthroughs.

2. **The Significance of Belief:** Jesus emphasizes the pivotal role of belief in manifesting our prayers. It's not merely about uttering words or making requests; it's about genuinely believing that our petitions will be fulfilled. Belief aligns our hearts and minds with God's will and activates

the power of faith within us. Wholehearted belief positions us to receive the fulfillment of our prayers.

3. **The Role of Prayer:** Jesus encourages us to present our desires before God in prayer. Prayer is an effective channel of communication with our Heavenly Father. It allows us to express our desires, seek His guidance, and align our hearts with His purposes. Through prayer, we invite God to work within and through us, trusting His wisdom and provision.

4. **The Promise of Answered Prayer:** God's Word assures us that our petitions will be granted when we pray with unwavering faith and belief. However, this promise is within the context of God's will.

As we contemplate Mark 11:23-24, let's recognize the potency of faith and prayer. Let's nurture unwavering faith, believing God can move mountains in our lives. In prayer, let's seek His will and trust in His provision. Let our wishes be in harmony with His intentions, trusting He listens to our prayers and responds according to His unfailing plan.

Prayer: Heavenly Father, I thank You for the profound lessons on faith and prayer from Jesus. Help me to cultivate unwavering faith, trusting that You can move mountains in my life. Guide me to align my desires with Your will and to trust in Your perfect timing. As I present my requests to You in prayer, grant me the assurance that You will answer according to Your purposes. Strengthen my faith and deepen my prayer life, allowing me to experience the transformative power of Your presence. In Jesus' name, Amen.

Insight: Reflect on Mark 11:23-24. How do these teachings on faith and prayer challenge or encourage you? Are there areas in your life where you need to exercise greater faith or align your desires with God's will? Spend time in prayer, surrendering your desires to God, seeking His guidance, and trusting in His faithfulness to answer your prayers according to His perfect plan.

Date: _____

Reflection or Thoughts:

(Start writing your reflections, thoughts, prayers, or anything you wish to journal about in the space below.)

_____
_____
_____
_____
_____
_____
_____
_____
_____
_____
_____
_____
_____
_____
_____
_____
_____
_____
_____
_____
_____
_____
_____
_____
_____
_____
_____

Day Thirty-Five: The Transformative Power of Faith and Worship

"About midnight Paul and Silas were praying and singing hymns to God, and the other prisoners were listening to them."
(Acts 16:25, NIV)

Further Reading: Acts 16:19-34

Good morning! Acts 16:19-34 recounts the inspiring account of Paul and Silas, imprisoned yet unwavering in their faith and devotion. Their fervent prayers and worship created an atmosphere for God's intervention—a seismic event that broke the prison's foundations and unshackled every captive.

Let's pattern the faith-filled prayers and worship that Paul and Silas offered to God. Let's create an environment for God's sudden response, freeing us from all bondage and setting the stage for God to do the extraordinary in our lives.

Reflect on the areas in your life where you feel imprisoned or bound. Are there chains hindering your progress? Are these chains self-imposed or outside of your control? Take a moment to bring these concerns before God in prayer.

Prayer: Dear Heavenly Father, I come before You, seeking liberation from the chains that bind me. Grant me the faith and determination of Paul and Silas to worship You despite difficult circumstances. Break the barriers and limitations holding me back, setting me free to fulfill Your purpose in my life. Amen.

Insight: Reflect on the transformative power of faith-filled prayer and worship. Consider sharing this experience with an accountability partner, inviting them to join you in prayer and fasting. The camaraderie between Paul and Silas proves that when we join our faith with others, we too can experience the miraculous as Paul and Silas did.

Date: _____

Reflection or Thoughts:

(Start writing your reflections, thoughts, prayers, or anything you wish to journal about in the space below.)

_____
_____
_____
_____
_____
_____
_____
_____
_____
_____
_____
_____
_____
_____
_____
_____
_____
_____
_____
_____
_____
_____
_____
_____

Day Thirty-Six: Embracing God's Unfailing Promise

"So do not fear, for I am with you; do not be dismayed, for I am your God. I will strengthen you and help you; I will uphold you with my righteous right hand." (Isaiah 41:10, NIV)

Further Reading: Isaiah 41:8-20

Good morning! Ever wake up feeling a bit uncertain about the day? Well, here's a reminder that God's got your back! He's totally committed to you. So, no need to worry—God's in the business of turning tough times into something amazing.

This year, why not make it a goal to soak in God's promises? Take a few minutes each day to think about how He's come through for you in the past, and let those thoughts guide your day. Trust me, it's a game-changer! So, let's dive into this year confidently, knowing that God's promises are like a roadmap for our lives.

Prayer: Dear God, I stand on Your promises of strength and transformation. Help me to trust in Your unwavering provision, knowing You will turn desolation into abundance. May I see Your hand at work in my life and rejoice in Your unfailing love. Amen.

Insight: Reflect on instances where you've witnessed God's transformative power. Share your experiences with someone to encourage and uplift them in their faith journey.

Allow God's promises to resonate in your heart, trusting in His provision and experiencing His transformative power in your life.

Date: _____

Reflection or Thoughts:

(Start writing your reflections, thoughts, prayers, or anything you wish to journal about in the space below.)

Day Thirty-Seven: Reviving Dry Bones through Faith and Prophecy

"The hand of the Lord was on me, and he brought me out by the Spirit of the Lord and set me in the middle of a valley; it was full of bones." (Ezekiel 37:1, NIV)

Further Reading: Ezekiel 37

Good morning! Today's passage from Ezekiel 37, the Valley of Dry Bones, reveals a profound vision of restoration and renewal granted to the prophet Ezekiel. It symbolizes God's power to breathe life into hopeless situations, reviving that which seems dead.

Imagine yourself standing in a metaphorical valley, surrounded by the dry bones of challenges and spiritual emptiness. Picture the desolation in your own life—those moments that feel barren or hopeless. Ezekiel's experience mirrors the struggles we all face at times. Take a moment to reflect on your own situations where you long for renewal and restoration. What are the areas in your life that resonate with the dry bones in Ezekiel's valley, where you seek a revival of hope and life?

As Ezekiel was commanded to prophesy over the dry bones, you have the authority through the blood of Jesus Christ to speak life into those desolate areas of your life. Take a moment to list what seems lifeless and lost, ready to pray, speak, and breathe God's life into these situations. *(Write down the list in the space provided on the next page).*

Prayer: Heavenly Father, I acknowledge the areas in my life that feel dry and lifeless. Please help me to speak. Today, I speak life, restoration, and renewal over these circumstances. Breathe Your life-giving Spirit into my situation and let Your divine restoration manifest in my life. Amen.

Insight: Consider how God can revive seemingly lifeless situations and how His restoration can bring forth new life. Believe in His ability to resurrect and renew that which appears impossible.

Date: _____

Reflection or Thoughts:

(Start writing your reflections, thoughts, prayers, or anything you wish to journal about in the space below.)

Day Thirty-Eight: Surrendering To God's Prevailing Purpose

"Many are the plans in a person's heart, but it is the Lord's purpose that prevails." (Proverbs 19:21, NIV)

Further Reading: Proverbs 19

Good morning! Think about a time in your life when things didn't go as planned, and you had to align with what you believed God wanted for you. It might have felt uncertain or tough at the moment, but Proverbs 19:21 speaks to those moments, highlighting that despite our plans, God's purpose takes precedence. Can you recall a situation where you had to navigate uncertainties by following God's lead instead of sticking to your initial plans?

Reflect on instances where God's purpose prevailed over your plans. Take a moment to write down what you sense God is calling you to or from, seeking His guidance in alignment with His will.

Prayer: Gracious God, help me surrender my plans to align with Your purpose. Grant me clarity and courage to follow Your guidance, even when it diverts from my plans. Let Your purpose prevail in my life, bringing fulfillment and peace. Amen.

Insight: Trust in God's greater wisdom and purpose, even if it challenges your plans. Seek His guidance through prayer and study, surrendering your will to His divine direction.

Let these reflections guide you in embracing God's restoration and purpose in your life, believing in His ability to revive and lead you according to His divine plan.

Date: _____

Reflection or Thoughts:

(Start writing your reflections, thoughts, prayers, or anything you wish to journal about in the space below.)

_____
_____
_____
_____
_____
_____
_____
_____
_____
_____
_____
_____
_____
_____
_____
_____
_____
_____
_____
_____
_____
_____
_____
_____
_____
_____
_____

Day Thirty-Nine: Trusting In Transition

"The Lord himself goes before you and will be with you; he will never leave you nor forsake you. Do not be afraid; do not be discouraged." (Deuteronomy 31:8, NIV)

Further Reading: Deuteronomy 31

Good morning! During times of transition, such as entering new phases in careers, relationships, or life changes, it's crucial to align ourselves with God's guidance. Deuteronomy 31:8 reassures us that God goes before us, remaining by our side, never forsaking or failing us.

Take a moment to ponder the following:

1. What are your true desires during this transition?

_____
_____
_____
_____
_____
_____
_____
_____
_____
_____
_____
_____
_____
_____
_____

2. Are you prepared for an introspective journey to discover your authentic path?

_____
_____
_____
_____
_____
_____
_____
_____
_____
_____
_____
_____

Consider where you are right now. Are you experiencing genuine joy in your life? Suppose your answers reveal a lack of joy or unfulfillment. In that case, it might signal the need for a significant shift toward joyful things— like stopping to smell the roses. Embrace the transition—it might be unsettling, yet essential for your growth. Know that the Lord stands with you, promising never to forsake you.

Prayer: Dear God, in times of transition, guide my steps. Grant me clarity in my desires and help me seek Your authentic path. As I navigate new territories, let Your presence be my assurance, knowing You'll never abandon me. Amen.

Insight: Acknowledge God's companionship during transitions, understanding that it's often a necessary phase toward greater fulfillment and purpose.

Date: _____

Reflection or Thoughts:

(Start writing your reflections, thoughts, prayers, or anything you wish to journal about in the space below.)

_____
_____
_____
_____
_____
_____
_____
_____
_____
_____
_____
_____
_____
_____
_____
_____
_____
_____
_____
_____
_____
_____
_____
_____
_____
_____

Day Forty: Finding Strength in Uncertain Transitions

"And I will harden Pharaoh's heart, and he will pursue them. But I will gain glory for myself through Pharaoh and all his army, and the Egyptians will know that I am the Lord." (Exodus 14:4, NIV)

Further Reading: Exodus 14:1-28

Good morning! Sometimes, in the midst of transitions, we find ourselves in uncertain and lonely spaces, questioning our decisions and paths. Exodus 14:1-28 narrates a story of perplexity and triumph—a narrative many can relate to in their personal lives.

Reflecting on this passage, consider your current journey and moments where confusion and loneliness overshadow your purpose. You might be walking a path that seems not to bear fruit. We can sink into isolation and sadness when things aren't manifesting as we would like. Transitions come with a myriad of tests and emotions.

In moments when you face uncertainty, prayerfully consider the following:

1. Have you faced moments where your path feels uncertain or confusing?
2. How have you managed feelings of isolation or confusion during transitions?

In times of despair, seeking solace and wisdom from the Scriptures can supply Insight and strength. Moses' story at the Red Sea offers crucial lessons:

1. Clarity comes through movement and obedience to God's instruction, even in confusion. Trusting God's leading despite unclear paths is vital.

2. Your uncertainty may be a strategic tool against the enemy, safeguarding your destiny and deterring false allies.

3. Sometimes, what pursues you is a catalyst for your rightful positioning.

4. Your adversaries have a deadline; their pursuit will end, delivering you to your promise.

5. Everything, including your trials, serves God's greater purpose, bringing glory to Him.

Prayer: Loving Father, in my moments of confusion and isolation, grant me clarity and strength. Help me trust Your strategic guidance and understand that my adversities serve Your purpose. May I find assurance in You, knowing victory is mine through Christ. Amen.

Insight: May these reflections fortify you in moments of uncertainty, reminding you that God's strategic guidance works wonders even in the thick of your confusion, and His purpose will prevail. You are an overcomer in His name.

Date: _____

Reflection or Thoughts:

(Start writing your reflections, thoughts, prayers, or anything you wish to journal about in the space below.)

Day Forty-One: Cultivating Unwavering Faith

"If any of you lacks wisdom, you should ask God, who gives generously to all without finding fault, and it will be given to you. But when you ask, you must believe and not doubt, because the one who doubts is like a wave of the sea, blown and tossed by the wind." (James 1:5-6, NIV)

Further Reading: Hebrews 11

Good morning! James 1:5-6 assures us that God generously grants wisdom to those who seek it without doubt. In life's journey, uncertainties often prevail, yet God's promises remain steadfast.

Let's consider these steps to reignite your faith and belief:

1. Reflect on what you're seeking from God. Be genuine and sincere in your desires.

2. Write your request and timestamp it, acknowledging your need for God's intervention.

3. Set a future date to revisit your request, expecting its fulfillment.

4. Spend 15 minutes in stillness with the Holy Spirit, visualizing the fulfillment of your requests.

5. Record your thoughts, recognizing them as crucial to fulfilling God's promise.

Prayer: Gracious Father, I humbly bring my heart's desires before You, seeking Your faithful and supernatural response. Grant me the wisdom and faith to trust in Your perfect timing. Amen.

Insight: Embrace this challenge to activate your faith anew. Believe, dream, trust, smile, love, and live again.

Date: _____

Reflection or Thoughts:

(Start writing your reflections, thoughts, prayers, or anything you wish to journal about in the space below.)

Day Forty-Two: Embracing Joy in Trials

"Consider it pure joy, my brothers and sisters, whenever you face trials of many kinds because you know that testing your faith produces perseverance. Let perseverance finish its work so that you may be mature and complete, not lacking anything."
(James 1:2-4, NIV)

Further Reading: James 1

Good morning! I don't know about you, but it is sometimes difficult to muster up even an ounce of joy when you face challenges and uncertainties. Yet embracing joy during trials is your safe landing card. Maintaining a posture of joy is exactly the anecdote for your breakthrough.

In the journey of life, trials and challenges are inevitable. Yet, James encourages us to find joy amid trials, understanding that they are opportunities for growth and the development of enduring faith. It's a perspective that goes against the natural inclination to view difficulties as setbacks.

Consider the trials you've faced in your life. Have they not, in retrospect, shaped you in profound ways? They are not just obstacles to overcome but instruments for refining your character and deepening your trust in God.

God's purpose in allowing trials is not to bring harm but to bring about maturity and completeness in us. As we navigate through challenges, God is at work, molding us into the image of His Son and equipping us for a life that reflects His glory.

Prayer: Heavenly Father, we come before You, acknowledging that trials are a part of our journey on this earth. Help us to embrace them with joy, knowing that You are using them to refine us and strengthen our faith. Grant us the wisdom to see beyond the difficulties and to recognize that growth comes from persevering through trials.

In moments of challenge, may we find our refuge and strength in You. Teach us to trust Your plans, even when we cannot fully comprehend them. May the testing of our faith produce perseverance, leading us to a place of maturity and completeness in Christ.

Thank you for the assurance that through every trial, You are with us, working all things together for our good. In Jesus' name. Amen.

Reflection Questions:

1. Can you recall a specific trial or challenge in your life that, in hindsight, brought about positive growth or transformation?

2. How can you shift your perspective to consider trials as opportunities for God to work in your life?

3. In what ways can you rely on God's strength and wisdom to navigate the trials you are currently facing?

Insight: As you reflect on these questions, may God's Word guide you and bring a renewed sense of joy in the knowledge that He is with you in every trial.

Date: _____

Reflection or Thoughts:

(Start writing your reflections, thoughts, prayers, or anything you wish to journal about in the space below.)

_____
_____
_____
_____
_____
_____
_____
_____
_____
_____
_____
_____
_____
_____
_____
_____
_____
_____
_____
_____
_____
_____
_____
_____
_____

The End

As we conclude this devotional journey, let's reflect on the transformation and growth experienced. Do not get fixated on big wins. Small wins and changes are to be celebrated, too. We delved into Scripture daily, prayed earnestly, and discovered strategies for navigating life's transitions.

This journey originated from my personal consecration and intimate moments with the Holy Spirit. My goal was to help guide you through unknown transitions. I pray you've felt God's hand mightily at work in your life during these 42 days, witnessing His faithfulness and wisdom as I have.

May the lessons learned stay with you as you seek God's face, trust His plans, and rely on His strength. Remember, God walks beside us, guiding each step. Return to these pages for encouragement and share insights with others. May this impact extend beyond the 42 days, fostering growth in your relationship with God.

Let us continue to experience God's transformative power, finding strength, peace, and joy in His presence. May your life testify to His faithfulness, and may you continually walk in His ways, experiencing His goodness.

With love,

Charlene

About the Author

Charlene Vassell-Wright is a remarkable woman who embodies the essence of living a purpose-driven life, guided by God's wisdom and fueled by a deep desire to impact others and help them navigate life's twists. She is a Certified Christian Life Coach with a stellar background as a highly experienced registered nurse. She began her nursing career at the University Hospital of the West Indies in Kingston, Jamaica. Driven by an unwavering commitment to serving others, Charlene is also an active missionary of Agape Missions International and the Founder and CEO of CVW Saving Lives Inc., a 501(c)(3) organization that focuses on empowering underprivileged youths and cultivating healthy minds to foster transformational leaders.

Charlene has organized and hosted women empowerment conferences, mental health programs, and conferences targeted to high school students and a successful 3-day retreat for teens in Ocho Rios, Jamaica. Charlene lives in Florida with her loving and supportive family.

Get inspired and empowered through her work, videos, blogs, coaching programs, workbooks, and other online products at www.cvwcoach.com. Through these resources, she aims to reach a wider audience and provide guidance and support to those seeking transformation and a deeper connection with their purpose.

Connect with Author

Stay connected at www.cvwcoach.com

Scan the QR code for direct access to the website.

Share how this devotional has impacted you by using the hashtag **#morningswiththeholyspirit42** and tagging **@charlenevassellwright** on Instagram.

www.ingramcontent.com/pod-product-compliance
Lightning Source LLC
Chambersburg PA
CBHW071147060526
44107CB00133B/344